Thaddeus Hyatt

The Prayer of Thaddeus Hyatt to James Buchanan

Thaddeus Hyatt

The Prayer of Thaddeus Hyatt to James Buchanan

ISBN/EAN: 9783743418912

Manufactured in Europe, USA, Canada, Australia, Japa

Cover: Foto ©Suzi / pixelio.de

Manufactured and distributed by brebook publishing software
(www.brebook.com)

Thaddeus Hyatt

The Prayer of Thaddeus Hyatt to James Buchanan

THE PRAYER

OF

THADDEUS HYATT

TO

JAMES BUCHANAN,

PRESIDENT OF THE UNITED STATES,

IN BEHALF OF KANSAS,

ASKING FOR A

Postponement of all the Land Sales in that Territory,

AND FOR OTHER RELIEF;

TOGETHER WITH

CORRESPONDENCE AND OTHER DOCUMENTS SETTING FORTH
ITS DEPLORABLE DESTITUTION FROM THE

DROUGHT AND FAMINE.

Submitted under oath, October 29, 1860.

———————

WASHINGTON:
HENRY POLKINHORN, PRINTER.
1860.

CONTENTS.

DISTRICT OF COLUMBIA, }
    City and County of Washington. }

    I hereby certify, that, on this 29th day of October, A. D. 1860, before the subscriber, a Notary Public in and for the county of Washington in the District of Columbia, personally appeared Thaddeus Hyatt, of the city of New York, and made oath that the statements hereinafter set forth are true to the best of his knowledge and belief; that he has no pecuniary interest in the question involved; and that this prayer is not made for any other purpose than for the relief of the unfortunate people of Kansas.

THADDEUS HYATT.

            Subscribed and sworn before me, this twenty-ninth [SEAL.]   day of October, in the year one thousand eight hundred and sixty.

JOHN S. HOLLINGSHEAD,
Notary Public.

LETTERS OF THADDEUS HYATT

ADDRESSED TO THE PRESIDENT, THE SECRETARY OF WAR,

AND THE SECRETARY OF THE INTERIOR.

———————•———————

WASHINGTON, *October* 29, 1860.

To PRESIDENT BUCHANAN:

SIR: As your verbal reply to my communications [see *infra*, A 1, A 2, A 3] of the 16th instant gave me no positive assurance that the land sales in Kansas will be postponed; and as your failure to give me this assurance seemed to rest upon a necessity for more authoritative and formal data for official action, I have delayed my departure from Washington in order to throw into a more convincing and satisfactory shape the materials in my possession. In addition to my own memoranda, I have also sent communications to the War Department and to the Secretary of the Interior asking information, as appears in the copy herewith submitted. [See *infra*, B and C.] I have as yet received no reply from those Departments. On the 18th instant I addressed a communication to Professor Henry, of the Smithsonian Institution, the reply to which and my own letter accompany this. [See *infra*, D and E.] It will be seen that his report exactly harmonizes with all the other testimony.

That your Excellency may understand the value of the array of facts which I herewith present under oath, permit me to say, that to collect them my journey through Kansas covered nearly one thousand miles, and occupied twenty-five days; that rising of two thousand persons met together at a series of meetings held in the counties mentioned below, the most of whom I saw, and whose statements I heard; that letters and petitions have been sent to me on behalf of the sufferers, signed by over eight hundred persons, and representing twice as many thousands; and that the counties already reported by organized committees with whom I am in communication, embrace nearly the whole region of Kansas south of the Kaw river, who are looking for relief to my efforts in their behalf, as fully appears in what follows.

That my present petition in behalf of these suffering people may be so moderate and reasonable as to command a positive and immediate assurance from the Executive that the whole of the threatened land sales shall be at once postponed, I ask respectfully in their name, that your Excellency will grant a contingent and temporary postponement of ninety days, to enable me still further to accumulate proof upon proof of the utterly impoverished condition of the people.

With the greatest deference to your Excellency, let me say that an array of facts such as is now presented by me here, and under oath, would, if presented in a Court of Chancery, be sufficient for obtaining an injunction in any case of a parallel character.

Yours, &c., respectfully,

THADDEUS HYATT.

A 1.

WASHINGTON, D. C., *October* 16, 1860.

To JAMES BUCHANAN,
President of the United States:

SIR: Having just returned from the Territory of Kansas, where I have been an eye-witness to the deplorable and

starving condition of that scorched and famine-stricken land,
I come to implore of the Executive, as an act of clemency in
behalf of its suffering inhabitants, that all Government lands
now offered for sale in that Territory may be withheld from
market, and more especially those lands embraced in what
is known as the New York Indian Reserve, (Proclamation
No. 667.)

You need be informed, sir, of but half the desolations and
heart-rending scenes I have witnessed among that heroic and
industrious, but unfortunate people, to arouse your utmost
sympathies.

Thousands of once thrifty and prosperous American citizens are now perishing of want. Winter is upon them; of
clothing they are nearly bereft; food they have not to last
them through the cold season that is approaching. Of over
a hundred thousand people upon Kansas soil six months ago,
at least one fourth or one third have left; of the remainder
it is safe to say that forty thousand at this moment see
nothing but exodus or starvation at the end of the sixty
days now just before them; from ten to twenty thousand
look with only despairing eyes upon November; thousands
connot subsist a month longer unaided; other thousands are
living upon the little which the neighbors deprive themselves
of to give to them — neighbors equally unfortunate, and
with whom the starvation is merely a question of but a few
days longer; while still other thousands, if not at once
relieved, must perish from hunger or the diseases that follow
in its train. Some have already died, others are daily dying;
while the hours grow darker and the days wax longer for
the living to whom relief comes not, and whose eyes are
aching with watchings for the succor that delays.

In confirmation of these frightful statements, I refer your
Excellency to the accompanying extracts from my diary
while in Kansas recently, and from numerous letters sent
to me from various districts of the famine-land.

Had the blood of this poor people in 1860 been as valuable

for coinage into votes as it was in 1856, your department would have long since been made aware of their miseries, and it would not have remained for the discharge of a mere mechanical duty to have brought to your notice the sickening fact that the mere performance of the duty was in its terrible workings a practical cruelty, such as no Despotism on earth would intentionally be guilty of, and such as, being once brought to the notice of your department, it cannot but rejoice to have escaped committing.

Commending these facts to your careful consideration, I have the honor, sir, to subscribe myself,

Very respectfully, yours,

THADDEUS HYATT.

A 2.

Washington, D. C., *October* 16, 1860.

To James Buchanan,
  President of the United States:

Sir: As the condition of Kansas admits of no delay, I have to request that the extracts herewith submitted for your Excellency's inspection — of which I cannot make copies in time for you to-day — may be returned to me this afternoon, together with your action thereon, as I leave in the morning for the East, to raise funds for the relief of these people.

I will, however, furnish you with copies of these and other documents, to be left on file, if desired.

Very respectfully, yours

THADDEUS HYATT.

A 3.

WASHINGTON, D. C., *October* 16, 1860.

Hon. JACOB THOMPSON,
      Secretary of the Interior:

SIR: In my interview with the President, as I have already informed you, yesterday, he desired me to procure from you the following data, viz:

1st. What amount of lands are offered for sale in (the New York Indian Reservation) Kansas?

2d. What is the urgency of the necessity for the sale?

By furnishing these data, and more especially by your favorable consideration of the accompanying appeal, and your favorable recommendation in the premises, you will perform an act of humanity, that will fill the hearts of thousands with gratitude towards yourself and the administration — while all the people, despite the asperity of party strife, will join in approbation of the act.

I have the honor to be, yours, sir, respectfully,

THADDEUS HYATT.

B.

WASHINGTON, *October* 24, 1860.

Hon. JOHN B. FLOYD,
      Secretary of War:

SIR: Being about to furnish the President with some statistics in reference to the unprecedented drought which has afflicted Kansas Territory for more than fourteen months, I have to request that you will favor me with replies to the following queries, viz:

1st. What amount of rain has fallen in that Territory during the last fourteen months?

2d. What has been the state of the atmosphere?

Together with such comments as you may deem proper to submit as to the causes of the existing famine in said Territory.

       I have the honor to be, sir, very respectfully,

THADDEUS HYATT.

C.

WASHINGTON, October 24, 1860.

Hon. JACOB THOMPSON,
       Secretary of the Interior:

SIR: Will you please answer the following queries? I wish to lay them before the President in the matter of the present application which I have made for the relief of the settlers in Kansas.

1st. What is the present population of Kansas as appears upon your records, county by county; when taken; and state the date when taken?

2d. What amount of corn and provisions were raised last year, county by county; when taken; date when taken?

3d. What amount of corn and provisions were raised this year, county by county; when taken; date when taken?

4th. What amount of corn and provisions have the people on hand for the coming winter, county by county; when taken; date when taken?

5th. What amount of money and moveable wealth was there in Kansas, and how distributed, county by county; when taken; date when taken?

6th. What amount of public lands are now offered, or about to be offered, for sale in said Territory, in what localities, and date of sales?

By furnishing the above from your census returns, &c., you will much oblige. &c.,

Very respectfully,

THADDEUS HYATT.

THE DROUGHT IN KANSAS.

D.—*Thaddeus Hyatt to Professor Henry, Secretary of the Smithsonian Institution.*

WASHINGTON, *October* 18, 1860.

SIR: Bing about to furnish President Buchanan with some statistics in reference to the unprecedented drought which has afflicted Kansas Territory for more than fourteen months past, I have to request that you will favor me with replies to the following queries, viz:

1st. What has been the average fall of rain in that Territory for the last ten years?

2d. What amount has fallen during the last fourteen months?

Together with such comments as you may deem proper to submit as to the causes of the existing famine in said Territory.

By so doing, you may contribute something to the relief of suffering thousands, and assist his Excellency in the discharge of an important duty.

I am, sir, very respectfully, yours,

THADDEUS HYATT.

Prof. HENRY, *Secretary Smithsonian Institution.*

E.—*Report of Professor Henry, furnished in reply to the request of Thaddeus Hyatt.*

SMITHSONIAN INSTITUTION,
Washington, D. C., October 25, 1860.

DEAR SIR: In answer to your letter of the 18th instant, I send you herewith —

The mean fall of rain for every month at Forts Atkinson,

Leavenworth, Riley, and Scott, from the Army Meteorological Observations.

The amount of rain at Burlingame and Manhattan, during a number of months in 1858, 1859 and 1860; at Neosho Falls in 1859 and 1860; and at Gardner from April to August, 1860, from our own records:

Also from our records, remarks on the drought in Kansas from the Meteorological Registers of G. F. Meriam, at Gardner, from April to September, 1860, and from the Register of B. F. Goss, at Neosho Falls, from July 1860.

It is evident from the facts thus furnished, that a severe drought has prevailed during the past season in Kansas Territory.

Very respectfully, your obedient servant,

JOSEPH HENRY, *Secretary.*

THADDEUS HYATT.

RAIN IN KANSAS.—*Furnished in answer to Letter of Thaddeus Hyatt, October 18, 1860.*

Station.	January	February	March	April	May	June	July	August	September	October	November	December	
Fort Atkinson	0.71	0.83	2.54	4.68	5.04	6.68	5.67	5.08	2.81	1.51	0.50	0.73	Mean of two years and one month — from May 1844, to May 1846.
Fort Leavenworth	0.72	1.01	1.61	2.74	3.62	5.80	3.15	3.29	3.32	1.84	2.17	1.02	Mean of eighteen years and two months —from May 1836, to July 1855.
Fort Riley	0.31	0.60	1.18	2.59	4.14	3.08	4.08	2.99	4.18	0.02	1.38	0.35	Mean of two years and two months— from November 1853, to Jan. 1855.
Fort Scott	1.92	1.18	1.79	3.70	7.08	8.13	4.55	3.69	2.30	2.66	3.43	1.69	Mean of ten years and two months— from January 1843, to March 1853.
Burlingame 1858		0.43	2.42	3.15	1.52	6.95	5.06	4.45	2.19	7.32	2.76	0.82	
1859	1.34	0.22	3.05	2.22	6.28	7.20	3.70	4.42	1.25	0.10			
1860				0.55	1.20	2.05	1.52	0.85					
Manhattan 1858	2.50	0.46		4.44	5.12	4.83	6.31	3.98	1.10	4.67	0.69	1.11	
1859	1.50	0.61	2.88	2.51	9.42	3.57	1.99	6.84	1.82	0.64	1.20	0.20	
1860				0.12	1.13	2.69	2.09						
Neosho Falls 1859			2.41	3.26	8.17	6.77	2.55	5.54	2.65	0.85	0.27	0.15	
1860		2.21	0.00	0.53	0.95	2.13	1.14	1.68					
Gardner 1860			1.45	0.25	3.89	1.12	1.31						

Extracts from the Register of G. F. Merriam, of Gardner, Kansas, for the year 1860.

April.—The first half of the month has been a continua-
of the long, dry weather which has prevailed to a great extent
since the 25th of September, 1859.

20th. Last night a heavy dew fell—the first this spring.
Heretofore there has not a particle of dew fallen; the air has
been too dry.

May.—3d. Thunder-shower early this morning. Only a
trifle of water fell at this place, but a belt a mile and one-half
in width, running from southwest to northeast, and five or
six miles southeast of here, was almost deluged. I was told
to-day that so much water fell that the dry ravines were
filled with running water three feet deep. At least five or
six inches of water must have fallen to produce such a result
in the present state of the soil.

The last day of this month, I learned, there were very
heavy rains to the westward of us, extending to within eight
miles of us. The prospect for a really good rain here looks
now as far in the future as ever. Farmers have good cause
to be discouraged at the long continued drought, for their
crops at present promise a total failure.

June.—4th. We have no dews of any account. In fact, we
have had but one or two thus far this year that would wet a
person's feet by walking in the grass. Previous experience
has been the reverse.

July.—Thermometer, in open air, on the 8th and 17th, at
100 deg.; 20th, 101 deg.; 18th, 104 deg.; 7th, 9th, 15th, and
21st, 105 deg. Mean of the month, at 2 p. m., 95.5. The
7th—very hot day—by far the hottest one of the season; the
mercury ran up to 130 deg. on being exposed to the sun's
rays.

31st. The past month has been the hottest I ever saw. The ground is parched ; corn suffers badly, and unless we soon get rain, all the corn planted early will amount to nothing. Scores of farmers are discouraged, and leaving the country. Our prospects for a *bad* crop are good. Wheat is harvested, and averaged from two to ten bushels per acre ; but such as there is, is of a first rate quality. Potatoes promise no return ; oats are almost a total failure, and the same of all other grains and vegetables.

Many of the best wells are failing, and some are entirely dry. The very best springs only, which reach the top of the ground, afford any water.

Some of the cattle a few miles from here are dying with what is called the dry murrain. Grass is short, but far better than most other sections of the country. We now have an abundance of green corn, tomatoes, musk and water-melons, &c., from *gardens* ARTIFICIALLY *watered!*

AUGUST.—The past month has been a continuation of our severe and protracted drought. The ground is so very dry that large fissures have been opened in almost all possible directions, as well on the tough sod of the unbroken prairie as on ploughed land.

All the small streams which flow from central Kansas are dried up, and none but the best springs and wells afford water. Stock suffers severely for want of water ; in fact, many have died from this cause alone. I have from good authority that along the banks of the Missouri river, from Nebraska down, plenty of rain has fallen, but this belt is of but an insignificant width. In the Territory I learn that heavy rains have fallen in some places, but not enough to make a full crop anywhere.

The general complaint of poor crops and fears of suffering come from all parts of the country. No hay or Hungarian grass of moment will be saved for feed this winter, but as a compensation the farmers are busily engaged cutting and

curing their corn-stalks. Large tracts of this year's grass
have been burned—probably set on fire by malicious persons
on purpose to see the fire or to ascertain whether green grass
would burn or not.   Hundreds of families have left for the
States, disgusted with their prospects of being able to secure
a crop; hundreds more will leave, but a great many will be
compelled to remain for want of means to travel. These
will suffer this winter for food, or have at best a miserable
existence until another year. Corn will, in this particular
neighborhood, be half a crop, but taken throughout the
Territory, probably less than one-fourth.

Potatoes are doing nothing but die. Sorghum sugar cane
has a fair growth, and as a consequence a great deal of molasses will be made. Buckwheat, the last hope of many of
the farmers, is too poor to amount to anything, and the same
may be said of turnips, &c.

Little, if any, fall wheat has been sown yet, and unless it
rains a very small crop will be put in the ground. Farmers
fear the chinch-bug, which has appeared in such vast numbers
as almost to surpass belief. Taking all in all, our future,
for at least one year, looks gloomy enough. No dews have
fallen this month. The last half of this month has been re-
markable for the number of small whirlwinds. None were
of sufficient force to destroy property, yet they showed a
strange state of the air.

The few small showers we have had were of no general
extent—all were confined to narrow belts or spots.

SEPTEMBER. All kinds of crops are past redemption now.
Corn-fields that the owners were flattering themselves would
yield twenty-five to thirty bushels per acre, on being picked
show the *cob* with kernels at distances varying from one-
fourth to one inch apart. Thus the hopes of many are
blasted for this year. Of wheat very little will be put in the
ground.

*From the Register of B. F. Cox, Neosho Falls, Kansas, for
July, 1860.*

The 7th and 11th, thermometer 114, the wind blew strong
from S. W.—hot and dry as the blast from a furnace—a reg-
ular sirocco. We were obliged to shut up our houses and
keep out of it the best way we could, and were nearly suffo-
cated. Bees and other insects crowded into the house in
large numbers and were perfectly torpid from heat; most of
them recovered and flew away in the evening.

*A Statement of the Destitution in various Counties, as
gathered on the spot by Thaddeus Hyatt, from Statements at Public Meetings, Letters, &c., and from other
sources.*

SHAWNEE COUNTY.

THE AUBURN MEETING.

At a meeting held at Auburn, Shawnee county, September 11, 1860, A. L. Winans, Esq., president, D. B. Emmet
secretary —

Jude Winans stated the objects of the meeting, describing
the wants and sufferings of the county; others more than
confirmed his picture of the dearth and distress.

Alexander Emmerson said, he had sowed wheat and the
hail had destroyed his entire crop; last year he raised forty
bushels of corn to the acre; there is not a bushel of old corn
in his neighborhood; many had left; the hail storm on the
31st July destroyed all the crops and a number of houses;
there had not been four inches of rain in thirteen months.

W. Johnson, near Auburn, sowed forty-two bushels of
wheat with lime, and realizes nothing; planted thirty acres of

2

corn; got stalks but no corn; forty acres of buckwheat and ten of potatoes, and has got *nothing from all.* In 1857 there was no rain from April till the last of August, and yet, he raised seventy-five bushels of corn to the acre; more than usual was planted this year, extra exertions were made, and no returns. There is not enough breadstuff in the neighborhood to serve two months; has traveled on the road, and could find no corn till he got to Stranger creek, in Leavenworth county; even there he found the worm in the corn.

William West, of Ridge, says he will raise a few nubbins; no corn, no wheat, no buckwheat; will not raise seed from anything he planted, in the last twelve months; he is raising fodder for cattle, but for bread and seed he did not know what he would do.

G. D. Lathrop, of Middle Branch, says he planted sixty acres of corn; sowed twenty acres of fall wheat, and ten of spring wheat, and will not average, from all, two bushels to the acre; and the average of the neighborhood will not be more than one bushel to the acre, instead of fifty bushels, as heretofore.

Dr. Gamble, of One Hundred and Ten creek, says the crops are a total failure, but it is healthy in his neighborhood.

Elder Winans says, the crops are a total failure; there is not even a half a crop of fodder.

Rev. James F. Holliday, says, he has traveled over a considerable portion of Shawnee county, a part of Osage, and Waubunsee counties, and he thinks there will not be a bushel to the acre, all the crops are failures; has seen no vegetables except a few cucumbers; many have left, and others are leaving; there is not food enough to do the people two months; and there is no money; few would leave if they could help it; many have borrowed money to buy land warrants and pre-empt their lands, and many will lose their claims. For land warrants on twelve months time they pay $250 and $265, and four per cent. a month after due. The troubles of the settlers have been brought on by Government forcing the land sales; only for that, the people might have withstood the drought.

John W. Brown, says he has been here since 1849; from forty acres in wheat has raised nothing; of one hundred in corn, the yield will not be one bushel to the acre. There are fifty families in this township that have not two dollars to the family, nor two bushels of corn, and nothing else. His usual crops have been fifty bushels to the acre; there is not food enough in the whole county for more than one month, if equally divided, and very few have money to buy it if it was for sale.

W. Overstreet, says that last year he raised eighty bushels to the acre; this year he has nothing.

Dr. Wood, on the Waukarusa, said there were but a few bushels of corn in his neighborhood, and there is about one thousand acres of corn that will not produce even a pound of fodder.

The Auburn Docket, of September 20, 1860, describing the destitution of the county, and devising means for relief, says:

"The course pursued by the Administration (in forcing the lands into market) has deprived them of their cash resources, and now that their crops have failed them, they have nothing whatever to depend on. But few can be found who have enough to supply them during the winter, while many are now nearly destitute. We even hear of families who are living upon the milk of a single cow. One woman in Anderson county, has already died of starvation. * * The destitution of the people in the Territory has not been over estimated; they are out of money, and their crops are an entire failure."

THE FIRST TOPEKA MEETING.

At a meeting held at Topeka, Shawnee county, September 12, 1860, Mayor Farnsworth president, J. Brockway, secretary—

Judge Alfred L. Winans said he had twenty-eight years experience in the West, and he never saw people in so bad a condition as they are at the present time in Kansas. The farmers had put in a succession of crops, and thousands of acres on the Waukarusa will not produce anything; a whole field of eighteen acres would not produce four loads of fodder. From Waukarusa he drove twenty-six miles without finding grass for his horse, and had to go to Baldwin city before he found any feed. The people in Kansas are the most industrious farmers he ever saw.

E. Baily, west of Williamsport, said his teams were idle for want of employment; could not get one dollar per day for hauling; the prospects for crops last spring were good; there is nothing now; he has planted forty acres of corn, and cannot find a mess of roasting ears without worms. He is about starting for the East, with a wife and seven children, and with fifty cents in his pocket; he has already sacrificed his property, except his wagon and oxen, for three dollars and fifty cents.

O. C. Nichols, two miles south of Topeka, says, he last year raised thirty bushels of corn to the acre; will have this year about one half a bushel; his neighbors, who had raised sixty bushels to the acre last year, will have nothing this year. The people are generally industrious; one third of the settlers have mortgaged their claims. There are fifty or sixty families in the neighborhood; two-thirds of them would leave if they could.

Horatio Fletcher says, he sowed twenty-five acres of wheat—it failed; planted sixty-five acres of corn—it will not average three bushels to the acre.

L. C. Wilmarth says, that he will realize from twenty acres of wheat and fifteen acres of corn, two loads of fodder; from five acres of garden produce, nothing but a small bed of radishes; and he has lost several hundred young fruit trees.

James Buchanan, a farmer, said he located with plenty of money; spent it in improvements on his claim; planted sixty acres of corn, from which he will not have fodder enough to winter two cows; has no provisions.

S. T. Walkley said he subsoiled his land last year; raised fifty bushels to the acre; this year planted ninety acres, and sowed in good season, also, ten dollars worth of garden seed; he will realize nothing but a little fodder.

Rev. C. C. Hutchison said he had traveled much, and confirmed the worst statements made in regard to the crops; five members of his church had to leave and go East or starve.

H. W. Martin, of Tecumseh, said all the crops were short in his neighborhood, as in the surrounding townships; destitution general.

Rev. J. A. Steel says, he planted eight acres of corn, and will not get enough to feed a goose; planted potatoes, and did not get back a potato. He is a knave or a fool who says the people are not in want.

J. B. Brockway says, he has thirty acres of corn on the new bottom; last year he raised forty bushels, this year he may get seven; and he is better off than his neighbors; in the corn he gets, there are worms; and he does not know a field of potatoes that will produce one potato to the acre; and no wheat worth cutting; not more than four inches of rain has fallen in eleven months. Land warrants are bought at a high price, on time, and four per cent. a month interest after due; many have mortgaged their claims; great many cannot live through the winter without aid.

Rev. F. P. Mountforth sowed thirty acres of wheat, and it produced but seven bushels. In the bounds of his travels the land will not produce two bushels to the acre, and that is worm-eaten.

A committee was appointed to solicit relief through Thaddeus Hyatt, as follows: John W. Brown, William Overstreet, Judge Winans, William West, Samuel Garrison, and Rev. F. P. Mountforth.

THE SECOND TOPEKA MEETING.

Pursuant to previous notice, a meeting of the citizens of Shawnee county was held at Museum Hall, in Topeka, on Saturday, September 22d, for the purpose of eliciting the facts in regard to the failure of the crops of the present season, and the necessities of the people occasioned thereby. The meeting was called to order by Dr. James Fletcher, on whose motion I. N. Roberts, Esq., was called to the chair. On motion of Rev. L. Bodwell, James Fletcher and H. G. Lyons were elected secretaries. The President explained the object of the meeting.

On motion, the persons present from the several townships were requested to report for the same.

Messrs. H. W. Martin, I. N. Roberts, Rev. H. P. Robinson, J. P. Greer, H. W. Curtis, and —— Campbell reported for Tecumseh township. There had been sown 833 acres of wheat, from which had been harvested 256 bushels; 2,591 acres of corn planted, which would yield about 3,537 bushels; 110 acres of potatoes planted, which would yield 11 bushels; 63 acres of buckwheat sown, which was a total failure; 26½ acres of beans planted, from which would be harvested 10 bushels; 41 acres of turnips sown, a total failure; 84 acres of Hungarian grass sown, which yielded 7 tons. There are 58 bushels of old wheat and 2,560 bushels of old corn in the township; 23 families had left, and several more were preparing to leave on account of the scarcity of provisions. Of those who remained, many would need assistance, or employment at fair wages, to maintain themselves against want.

Messrs. Hiram Shields, R. O. Johnson, and H. G. Lyons reported for Monmouth township. 301 acres of wheat sown, and 14½ bushels raised; 1,339 acres of corn planted, which would yield 400 bushels; 34½ acres of potatoes planted, 56½ acres buckwheat sown, 10 acres of beans planted,

40 acres of Hungarian grass, 5½ acres of turnips sown, all of which were an entire failure. There are 1,200 bushels of old corn in the township; 21 families had left, and 6 more preparing to leave on account of the great scarcity of provisions for themselves and feed for their stock. Some 40 families remained, most of whom will need assistance or employment by which they can earn something to sustain themselves through the winter.

W. E. Bowker, John Plilly, and James Hunter reported for Soldier township. 200 acres of wheat sown, and 40 bushels harvested; 1,089 acres of corn planted, and 500 bushels raised; 20 acres of potatoes planted, which would yield nothing. There are 1,000 bushels of old corn in the township; 2 families had left, 65 families remained, most of whom, if they could get employment at fair wages, would be able to maintain themselves against want — otherwise they would need assistance.

Harvey J. Loomis reported for Mission Creek. There had been sown, and planted, in wheat, corn, buckwheat, potatoes, and beans, about 1,000 acres, from which had been raised 15 bushels of wheat, and some corn fodder—everything else an entire failure. Fourteen families had left on account of drought and scarcity of provisions; thirty-five families, from necessity or choice, remained, most of whom, if they could get employment, would be able to take care of themselves — some would need assistance. Six hundred bushels of old corn and some stock were the only available means in the settlement.

W. H. Overstreet, R. M. Fish, D. B. Emmett, and Wm. Atwood were present from Auburn township, but were not prepared to give the statistics of the township. They all corroborated each other in the statement, that the farmers had planted more, and cultivated with greater care than any previous year, and that it was an entire failure. About one hundred families were in the township, many of whom had no available means, and would need help.

George B. Holmes reported for Williamsport. The farmers in that settlement had sown and planted in wheat, corn, potatoes, beans, &c., all the land they had under cultivation, amounting to about one thousand acres, and raised nothing—every thing proved a failure.

James Fletcher reported for Topeka township. 1,540 acres of wheat sown, 110 bushels raised; 2,500 acres of corn planted, which would yield 750 bushels; 100 acres of potatoes planted—none raised; 150 acres of buckwheat sown—none raised; 35 acres of beans planted—none raised; 12 acres of turnips sown—none raised; 100 acres of Hungarian grass sown, which yielded 3 tons. There are 12 bushels of old wheat, and 1,300 bushels of old corn in the township; 19 families had left, and more were preparing to go; some would need help; most of the settlers could maintain themselves if they could get employment at fair wages.

Several persons stated that owing to the short time between the call and the meeting, their reports were imperfect, and many details of interest were entirely omitted, and that a strict investigation of all the facts, and especially the wants of the people, would show a more distressing state of affairs than had been reported to the meeting.

On motion, the reports were referred to a committee consisting of one from each township, with instructions to arrange them in an abstract form, and send the same to Mr. Hyatt. The committee consisted of James Fletcher, of Topeka, Rev. H. P. Robinson of Tecumseh township, Geo. B. Holmes of Williamsport, J. W. Brown of Auburn, H. G. Lyons of Monmouth township, and James Hunter of Soldier township.

On motion of H. C. Hawkins, the townships were requested to appoint township relief committees, and the chairman of each township committee to be constituted a member of a county relief committee, and report the same to the secretary of this meeting on or before two weeks next Wednesday.

On motion, the meeting adjourned.

I. N. ROBERTS, *President.*

JAMES FLETCHER, }
H. G. LYONS, } *Secretaries.*

The following is the report above referred to, condensed and presented in a tabular form, and forwarded to me by the chairman of the above committee:

ABSTRACT STATEMENT

Of Lands Planted and Crops Raised in Shawnee County, Kansas Territory, A. D. 1860.

Townships.	Wheat sown.	Wheat raised.	Corn planted.	Corn raised.	Potatoes planted.	Potatoes raised.	Buckwheat sown.	Buckwheat raised.	Beans sown.	Beans raised.	Turnips sown.	Turnips raised.	Hung'n grass sown.	Hung'n grass raised.	Old wheat on hand.	Old corn on hand.
	Acres.	Bush.	Acres.	Bush.	Acres.	Bush.	Acres.	Bush.	Acres.	Bush.	Acres.	Bush.	Acres.	Tons.	Bush.	Bush.
Topeka	1540	110	2500	750	100	—	150	—	35	—	12	—	100	3	12	1300
Monmouth......	301	14½	1339	400	34	—	56	—	10	—	5	—	40	—	—	1200
Soldier..........	200	40	1089	500	20	—	—	—	5	—	3	—	—	—	—	1600
Mission Creek..	80	15	800	—	15	—	15	—	—	—	—	—	—	—	—	600
Tecumseh	833	256	2591	3537	110	11	63	—	26	10	41	—	84	7	58	2560
Williamsport...	—	—	—	—	—	—	—	—	—	—	—	—	—	—	—	—
Auburn..........	—	—	—	—	—	—	—	—	—	—	—	—	—	—	—	—
Total	2954	435	8319	5187	279	11	284	—	76	10	61	—	224	10	70	6660

WILLIAMSPORT TOWNSHIP.—The farmers sowed to wheat, turnips, buckwheat, Hungarian grass, and planted to corn, potatoes, and garden vegetables, all the lands in the settlement, amounting to about 1,000 acres, and raised nothing—neither grass, roots, or grain of any kind.

AUBURN TOWNSHIP.—The report of this township was sent by the township committee direct to Mr. Hyatt; hence we can only report that its condition is like the other townships in the county, and the crops are an entire failure.

The foregoing report of Shawnee county is necessarily very imperfect, owing to the limited notice given. Many farms are not reported, and many details of interest are entirely omitted. We are, however, informed that garden vegetables have been an entire failure. Chinese sugar cane was planted on many farms, and except in Tecumseh township, and a small portion of Topeka township, is reported a failure, where it is estimated 500 gallons of molasses will be made. By the above report it will be seen that there was planted and sown in the county (making a fair estimate for Auburn township) 17,500 acres, from which has been raised 435½ bushels of wheat, 5,187 bushels of corn, 11 bushels of potatoes, 10 bushels beans; add estimate 500 gallons molasses, 10 tons Hungarian grass, and you can see all the products of our farms for the year 1860. It is estimated that 100 families have left the county, and as many more must leave, or have immediate aid, by donations or employment, which they cannot at present procure; and nearly our entire stock of cattle and horses must be driven out of the territory to winter.   JAMES FLETCHER,
Chairman of Committee.

TOPEKA, *Shawnee county, September* 22, 1860.

BRECKINRIDGE COUNTY.

THE MEETING AT ITALIA.

At a meeting held at Italia, Neosho Rapids, Breckinridge county, September 7, 1860—

Jacob Kisling, of Jackson township, said that there had

not fallen five and a quarter inches of rain in eleven and a quarter months, as he had accurately measured it. He had planted corn, and would not get seven bushels to the acre, where last year he raised forty-eight. Of all other crops he will have nothing.

Uriah Carter, of Weller creek, said he has planted corn on ground that last year produced about sixty bushels to the acre, and this year he will get no corn and but little fodder. No one in his neighborhood, except Mr. Ashpole, has raised any corn this year, and he, out of forty acres, will get but ten bushels an acre from five acres—all the rest will yield but fodder. There is not enough corn to do the people two months. Potatoes are dead. Some families have left, others are unable to go. There is no money and no provisions; only a little meat in the neighborhood. There is a settlement of Norwegians on Fall river, twenty miles south of Willow, who have scarcely anything, and no means to get away. They must suffer, if not soon relieved. There is not in that vicinity one bushel of flour to one family in fifty. Great sacrifices have been already made. *Had the land sales which took place a short time since been postponed,* the people would have had some means to get through the season.

Judge A. J. Mitchell, of Jackson township, said that out of sixty acres in corn, from ten to fifteen will produce from five to ten bushels to the acre—the remainder will give nothing but fodder, which would not be fit for use in a good season. No wheat, no potatoes; and if it does not rain he will have no buckwheat. This was the picture of the country near him.

Mr. Baily said he had fifty acres in corn last year, on which he raised more corn than he will get from two hundred acres this year. In good seasons the yield will be from eighty to one hundred bushels to the acre, and corn will grow here without rain as well as in any country in the world. Will have some turnips, if it rains; [*no rain fell.*] There is grass and fodder enough to feed the cattle, but some of the hogs must "root, or die." Calves are dying with the black-legs.

Samuel Van Gundy, on the bottom in Jackson township, said he had eighty acres of corn. Seven acres will yield about thirty bushels, the rest five bushels to the acre. He has plowed his wheat up and planted it in corn. There is no corn upon the upland farms, and the worms are in the bottoms.

Sylvester Adams, of Jackson township, had twenty acres in corn, which will yield ten or twelve bushels to the acre. The people have nothing but corn; and no money—all used to pay for land.

Alexander Baily says he sowed spring wheat, and sixteen acres of fall wheat; raised nothing. Ploughed it up and put in buckwheat, and if he gets his seed he will do well. Of eighty acres of corn, the average will be one bushel to the acre—all old ground except ten acres. Last year averaged thirty bushels. There is little old corn in his neighborhood. His corn is losing every day, and he is cutting it up to save the fodder. Such is his neighborhood, where the cattle are dying of Spanish fever.

Dr. G. J. Tallman says he thinks the people in his vicinity may have enough for themselves, but nothing to spare for other neighborhoods.

Mr. Fennemore, northwest corner of Coffee county, says that there will be half a crop in the valley, and one-fourth of a crop of corn out of it. All other crops entire failures, except buckwheat, and that will be slim. Good husbandry has nothing to do with the failure, as all are alike, and there has been no lack of industry, but the very opposite. Crops till this year have been good. Lands have been mortgaged, and claims will be lost.

THE MEETING AT EMPORIA.

At a meeting held at Emporia, Breckinridge county, September 8, 1860, and largely attended, Dr. J. H. Watson chairman, and J. W. Randall secretary—

Messrs. N. Bixler, R. H. Abraham, J. M. Miller, of Fremont township; Dr. Hunt, John Triggs, Joel Haworth, and James Jackson, of Pike township; R. W. Cloud, of Waterloo township; John Fowler, Dr. C. C. Slocum, John Hammond, J. P. McElfresh, and James W. Randall, of Emporia township, and others, stated the condition of the people in their respective townships.

A report of a meeting held the night previous in Jackson township, was read.

In Fremont township it was agreed that there are not over 300 bushels of old corn, and the new crop will not produce on an average over two bushels to the acre; the wheat, oats and potatoes nearly a total failure, and the buckwheat destroyed by grasshoppers.

In Pike township, but two men had old corn to sell. This township is the most productive in the county, (as stated by the chairman.) It has more bottom land than any other township. The new crop will yield an average of one or two bushels to the acre, it being injured by grasshoppers and worms. Wheat and other crops were a total failure. Several families have left this township, and others preparing to depart.

Jackson township reported an average of about ten bushels of wormy corn to the acre on the bottom land; scarcely fodder on the upland. The old and new corn of that township will not more than furnish bread for its population.

Americus township (as reported by Thomas H. Stanley and Judge Baker) has not corn for its inhabitants. This joins the Kaw reservation, and they stated that there are

300 whites and about 900 Indians in that section who will not have half corn enough to bread them till next spring.

In Emporia township, a general failure of crops except corn, and that will not produce more than the fourth of a crop, and it will be generally wormy. Men have already worked two days for a bushel of corn. It was stated that last year many farmers raised 75 bushels of corn to the acre, and the universal testimony was that Kansas can withstand drought better than any of the States from which the settlers came. The testimony of all was that the people of this country were generally very industrious and persevering in their endeavors to raise crops. Last fall they sowed winter wheat; this they plowed up and put in spring wheat and oats; that not coming up, they planted it in corn, and in some instances re-planted; and lately buckwheat has been sown, which bids fair to be blasted and unproductive.

In some portions of this county the cattle disease has prevailed. In Emporia township about 70 head of choice cattle have died within the last three weeks.

It was stated that money was very scarce, and that stock could not be sold for money; and that owing to the land sales many had to use their last dollar to save their claims, and that a considerable number borrowed money and mortgaged their land, expecting to pay it out of this year's crops.

Judge Graham of Madison county, Myrock Huntley of the Verdigris, H. J. Barton of Butler county, A. E. Rhodes of Ottoe and Hunter counties, and A. Studebaker of Chase county, gave statements of the crops in those counties, which represent the people in a worse condition than in Breckinridge county.

After the statements were concluded, a committee of two persons from each township was appointed to obtain additional statistics, to seek out the destitute, and to report the same to Thaddeus Hyatt as soon as possible. The committees were as follows: Pike township, James Jackson and Dr. F. G. Hunt; Fremont, P. B. Maxson, J. M. Miller; Ame-

ricus, George Shockley, W. E. Denison; Emporia, G. D.
Humphrey, W. O. Ferguson, Joseph Hall; Jackson, Dr. G.
J. Tallman, H. S. Sleeper.

THE WATERLOO MEETING.

At a meeting held at Waterloo, Breckinridge county,
September 10th, 1860, R. W. Cloud president, John Way-
man secretary—

Sylvester Hill, north of Santa Fe road, said he planted
18 acres of corn and will only get about two loads of fodder.
Buckwheat and beans are killed, and no prospect for potatoes—last year he raised forty bushels to the acre, this year
a total failure. There has been no rain to soak the ground
since 1859. The corn-fields have been given up to the stock.
There is no corn in the neighborhood for bread. Land warrants are bought on time for $235, with 4 per cent. per
month after due. There about sixty families in this neighborhood in this fix. Five families have left, others will go
if they can. In Ohio, with such a drought, no green thing
would have been seen.

Albert Watkins says he has lived six years in the Territory, has raised heretofore 4,000 bushels of corn on 40 acres;
this season he may, from 90 acres, get 200 bushels of *corn
and worms together*; from 50 acres of wheat sowed, not a ker-
nel; his buckwheat, turnips, and beans are all a failure; had
sold most of his old crop—has only 100 bushels of old corn
left, and cannot sell his stock at any price. This is the general condition of his neighborhood. There will not be 50
bushels of córn raised in his township, north of the Santa Fe
road. Near Waterloo the cattle were dying of the Texas
fever.

J. D. Wiggins, of Duck Creek, said he had planted 10
acres of corn and one of garden produce—got no corn, and
nothing but a saucer of peas. There are ten families on the
Creek, and only one has corn enough to bread them; many
cattle had died, others are diseased.

LINN COUNTY.

At a meeting called and held in Mound City, August 30, 1860, of representatives from the various townships of that county and some from counties along the southern line of Kansas, the following statements, among others, were made. The condition of this county may be taken as a fair illustration of the true situation of the whole Territory.

David Reese, one of the old settlers, says: "Things are worse now than they were in 1856. Then we had money; now we have none. I believe that if all the money in Linn was distributed out even, it would not count three dollars to a man. I have been here since early in '56, and gone through the troubles then; was taken prisoner and dragged away from my family; saw my neighbors' houses burnt and robbed —but, sir, this hour is a darker one for Kansas than even that! The crops are au entire failure. I planted twenty-four acres of corn, and will not get twenty-five bushels. There is not a vegetable in my garden. Everything is gone. Over there [pointing to a neighboring farm] lives an Illinois farmer. He came in here with ten thousand dollars in '57, and has a splendid farm; to-day he cannot command cash enough to pay trifling debts. He understands farming well, and has put in one crop after another in succession, hoping for rain with each one, but all have failed. He has now gone to Missouri with some cattle to sell for ready money. We regard him as one of our rich men, and yet he is that hard up for cash. Down on Mine creek I know of eighteen families who have left for the States within the past week."

Dr. Samuel Ayers, who has traveled in the north portion of Linn, the south portion of Lykins, and to the east line of Anderson county, says: "There will be almost universal destitution. There are about three thousand bushels of old corn in that whole extent of country. In a short time it will be so that the people cannot get corn at all; unless aided, they cannot live. Their general fare now is nothing but corn bread and water. Crops were put in, but they have failed. I planted twenty-five acres of corn, but shall not get four bushels of corn from the whole of it. The corn will produce scarcely fodder enough for the stock. There is not corn enough to feed the hogs. Wheat and spring crops are an entire failure. The sick cannot get medicine, nor can they get such food as they require. I have expended all my means for medicines, and cannot now supply the demands upon me. In the west portion of the county, where the lands were last year ordered to be sold, the destitution is peculiarly great, because the people have no money, and they have no money because they *were last year forced to pay for their lands.* Many of the poor settlers had no alternative but to mortgage their claims to raise the money demanded of them by the Government. The drought has come, and *pay day has come!* These poor people, unable even to subsist, and quite unable to pay borrowed money, will be driven from their claims, and lose all. Had we a homestead bill, this state of things could not exist."

Josiah Lamb, Potosi township, Mine creek, from ten acres of planted wheat, raised nothing; from sixty acres of corn he will realize nothing but fodder—not a roasting ear; has 100 bushels of old corn, and in that respect is better off than his neighbors; twelve families left his neighborhood during the last week; for land warrants and pre-emption claims the people are paying heavy interest and sacrificing their improvements.

J. H. Wilson, farmer, has twice planted forty-seven acres this season, and would sell his whole crop for two dollars.

Theodore Wilson, farmer, Mound city township, from forty-four acres planted in corn, potatoes, and other vegetables, he will have but fodder for his stock, and this is the general condition of his neighbors.

J. C. Holmes, Potosi township: Has not seen any corn

without worms.   The crops are a failure along the Missouri State line—people industrious—corroborates Stillwell's letter.

Rev. J. S. Swagerty, says, there are not four hundred bushels of corn on Lost creek; no wheat raised, and not corn enough to bread the families; the people are industrious and worked hard, yet many have sacrificed their claims and left.

Rev. Reuben Lamb, Potosi township, corroborating the above, adds, that cattle are dying of "Spanish fever;" the people are moral and industrious; would have been prosperous but for the drought. The sorghum is the only thing that has yielded even half a crop.

Rev. William Phillip: The grass is burnt, the corn is withered, where he had been in Lykins and Coffee counties, even up to the Santa Fe road; the people of Lykins county held a meeting to devise means to keep them from starving this coming winter.

Elder Hobbs, Baptist minister, corroborates the statements of distress and destitution in Allen, Anderson, Linn and Bourbon counties; many will lose their claims.

Thomas Jones, Mound city township, corroborates. the statements of Elder Hobbs; many will leave; others are unable to go.

Mr. Converse: The corn crop will not average over five bushels to the acre.   Buckwheat, turnips, and garden produce all failed.   The county is destitute.

Mr. Winship corroborates the above.

Mr. Davenport says, bread will be wanting; there will be need of seed spring wheat and corn.

C. Wheaton, farmer, has traveled over the territory ; many families are leaving, because they have not provisions ; the cattle are dying; on a portion of the Osage, people must starve if they are not supplied; the want is owing to the drought, and not from want of industry.

H. A. Smith, lawyer: There is an impression that a confession of the true condition of the people will lessen the price of lots; but it is better to stare the truth in the face, and make known our wants and be relieved.

Dr. Jennison: I have traveled some through the country, and seen enough to confirm the statements made here. When a traveler stops at a cabin, and the poor woman is an hour getting him something to eat — and then it is nothing but water, and corn-bread made of meal and water, and but little of that — you may judge that something is the matter with the people. As many as can go are getting away, and I know of some who have left without even the few shillings necessary to pay ferriage across the Missouri.

Jonathan Lyman, printer: Has not this season seen anything green but two messes of corn; he affirms the bankrupt condition of the people and failure of the crops.

Andrew Stark, farmer, says there will be required seed and corn for spring planting; one third of the citizens are leaving the county.

Chas. Clark, of Paris township, planted twenty acres of corn, and will not raise enough for his wife and child.

Mr. Blanchard, farmer, Turkey creek, planted sixty acres in corn, and will not raise anything; fourteen families southwest of Mound city township, have left.

L. Whitney, assessor: Not enough corn to keep the people until spring; few fields that yield much.

Eli Babb, county clerk, says, of twenty-five thousand acres put in corn this season, there will not be enough in the county to keep the people.

Solomon Mason, Paris township, planted seventy acres of corn; will not have a bushel to the acre; one tract of three hundred acres, that yielded five thousand bushels last year, will not average one bushel to the acre.

Father Cummings, from the north portion of Potosi township, said: "I planted sixty acres of corn, and out of it will get four acres of nubbins; the balance is nothing but fodder. There is not enough corn in the neighborhood to supply bread. The beans are promising, but the prairie chickens are eating them up."

Rev. Mark Robinson: Endorses Stillwell's letter to the New York Tribune, even the cooking of eggs by heat of the sun; has traveled extensively over the territory on the Verdigris, Walnut creek, Fall river, Butler, Hunter, and Greenwood counties; the crops are an entire failure; the people are industrious; have put in crop after crop and all have failed.

George Burchard confirmed the Stillwell letter. Mr. and Mrs. Stillwell being present, reiterated its truthfulness, as did also several of their immediate neighbors from Mine creek.

It was "resolved" by this meeting of the people of Linn, that,

"The statement of wants and destitution in this vicinity, and the necessity of assistance, made by S. C. Stillwell, Esq., through the columns of the New York Tribune, is, in the judgment of this meeting, essentially correct."

Dr. Danforth corroborated the general destitution, and moved for a committee of relief, which was appointed.

The following is the report of the census taker, as furnished by Mr. Babb, the county clerk:

Number of farms	600
Improved land	28,000 acres.
Unimproved land	78,000 "
Corn raised in 1859	375,381 bushels.
Oats	8,575 "
Potatoes...................................	10,801 "
Buckwheat	2,979 "
Beans......................................	752 "
Sweet potatoes.............................	541 "
Wheat......................................	not reported.
Sorghum molasses...........................	9,441 gallons.

On hand June, 1860—

Old corn...................................	32,000 bushels.

Number of horses	1,477
Number of mules	85
Number of milch cows....................	1,695
Number of oxen	1,415
Number of other cattle....................	2,227
Number of hogs	7,600
Number of inhabitants....................	6,433
Number of voters	1,500

NOTE.—In the above report I have quoted the bushels of corn on hand June 1st, at thirty-two thousand. My figures, copied from the book of the county clerk, read thirty-two *hundred;* but, fearing an error, I have put it at thirty-two thousand, to avoid a seeming disposition to make a picture overdrawn. Even thus, the picture is bad enough, for upon the assumption of thirty thousand bushels of corn in Linn county, and presuming that there remains of last year's crop twenty thousand bushels—say fifty thousand bushels in all— we find, that to give to each person of the population the bare allowance of a slave, one peck per week, and make no account of the *et ceteras* allowed him in addition, this corn would support the population but till next June, even if they could live on it alone, and this upon the supposition that the few who have divide with the many who have not. But this is not supposable. Let us, therefore, call the *et ceteras* equal in value to one-third the peck per week of corn ; there is then but corn enough to barely keep the people alive till the 1st of next March, even upon the agrarian principle, while the cattle are left unprovided for ; and it would require more corn than they have got to fatten the swine alone.

ANDERSON COUNTY.

At a meeting held in Anderson county, September 1, 1860, Joseph Eaton, Esq., chairman, B. F. Ridgway secretary —

Many spoke, and from various statements of the farmers present, the probabilities are, that not more than five bushels of corn will be realized to the acre, and that of an inferior quality. Mr. Jones, the census taker, said, that "he had visited every cabin in the county. In Walker township, Anderson county, he found an entire family living on the milk of a single cow, having nothing else to subsist upon. In Ozark township, in a single section, he found five families living on nothing but corn bread and water, while another family of four were subsisting entirely on the milk of one cow, with nothing whatever to eat." He also said that he found actual starvation. One woman had really starved to death. A neighbor testified to the fact, acknowledging that their own wants had blinded them to the poor woman's actual condition until the hour for her relief had passed, and it was too late to save her. He also stated that he traveled for two days over a region so entirely destitute, that he could get nothing to eat himself, nor anything for his beast, except grass; and that in the entire county of Anderson, in which, to-day, the crops are more promising than any other county in Kansas, except Leavenworth, Doniphan, and Atchison, there is but two hundred bushels of wheat; that there will be neither potatoes nor other vegetables, and that the county will not this year raise half enough corn to support her population, the old being added in.

It is represented by Judge Arny, who resides in this county, that it has a population of 2,403 persons, 467 farms, 107,677 bushels of corn raised in 1859.

This old corn has nearly all been used up, and much of the new corn is so wormy that it cannot be used for bread, and is not even fit to feed to horses.

W. Q. Wickersham, of Ozark township, reports for the same, as follows:

Names of families who require help on Osage, Anderson county:

B. Butler, no crop; two yoke cattle, two horses, one wagon, one cow.

A. P. Horton, no crop; one yoke cattle, one cow.

Mr. McMullen, no crop; no stock; has promise of work, but no clothing for his family.

A. Daly, no crop; one cow, two horses, no other means; destitute.

J. Mills, no crop; one yoke cattle; no other means.

DEER CREEK.

John Volk, no crop; two horses, one wagon; no other means.

G. W. Temple, no crop; one cow, two horses and wagon; nothing else.

L. M. McComb, no crop; two cows, one yoke cattle; no other means.

Franklin Hull, no crop; two yoke cattle, one cow; no other means.

Mr. Hook, one yoke cattle, three cows; no other means.

Two unknown families, (forgot their names,) three yoke cattle, one span horses; out of provisions and means, and have been sick.

There is no sale for stock nor labor to perform.

This township is comparatively favorable.

ALLEN COUNTY.

At a meeting, held at Humboldt, on the Neosho, September 4, 1860, Dr. Miller chairman, J. H. Signor secretary, the following facts appeared:

Mr. Stewart, of Cottage Grove township, said that a large amount of wheat was sown last fall on the Neosho bottoms, and well put in, but not a bushel was realized from it. Upon the same ground spring wheat was sown, which also failed; then oats, which failed also; then Hungarian grass, which will produce less than a quarter crop. From thirty acres of corn he will not have in all thirty bushels. One neighbor has forty acres, from which he may get two bushels to the acre. Buckwheat was largely sown, but promises next to nothing; upon one-third of an acre, which last year yielded one hundred and thirty bushels of potatoes, this year he does not expect ten bushels. There are not one hundred bushels of old corn in the township: and not a man who could give even board for work. No soaking rain has fallen for fourteen months past.

Richard Jackson said, there is not corn enough in my neighborhood to bread the people, and they have no money to buy it with. Six families near Osage city have left because they could get no provisions, and numbers of other families would leave if they could.

B. B. Vining, of Owl Creek, Humboldt township, said that he had examined the corn in his neighborhood, and his opinion was that there may possibly be on an average *one bushel* to the acre. Potatoes are alive, and that is all. Knows of families now that are destitute. This morning saw a number who were starting for the East, who had actually no provisions to take with them for the way. The cattle disease, too, has been very bad. One man has lost six head, and has fifteen more that are sick. Another neighbor has lost three oxen out of four yoke, and had two more then sick. And the people generally have no money to pre-empt their lands with.

E. Young, of Humboldt township, said: "I have lived here five years. Last year I raised, on bottom land, forty bushels corn to the acre, where this year upon the same ground, I shall not get one bushel to the acre."

Lyman Rhodes, of Coffachique township, said: "I have one hundred acres of ground, which has been plowed and planted three times this season, to no purpose. First wheat, then corn, then turnips—all lost. In four acres planted with potatoes, I cannot find the first one. Sorghum is doing tolerably well. Last year upon the same ground had forty bushels corn to the acre. In favorable seasons, the land produces as well as Illinois. 'Spanish fever' has carried off many cattle in the neighborhood of Iola."

James A. Hunt reported sixty head of cattle as dead and dying with "Spanish fever" on Owl creek; also a suffering family of eight persons—six children and the parents, and others whom he knows of that will require aid.

The meeting appointed N. B. Blanton and J. B. Hunt a committee to report to Mr. Hyatt on the condition of Humboldt township. These gentlemen, on the 18th September reported as follows:

"One hundred families in this township will need seed wheat—four bushels to the family, four hundred bushels in all; two bushels of seed corn each, making two hundred bushels in all; the same number of bushels of potatoes; food also will be needed for thirty-five families for eight months; and before the first of April next the number of needy families will probably be increased."

BOURBON COUNTY.

At a meeting held on the Little Osage 29th September, 1860, (W. R. Griffith, from the Marmaton river, neighborhood of Fort Scott, chairman; H. Knowles, of the same place, secretary,) the following statements were made by citizens of Bourbon county:

Mr. Anderson, farmer, says that he has forty-five acres of corn, the best in the township, and it will not average three bushels to the acre. In three weeks one-fourth of the people of the township will leave; half that want to go have not the means. There is not one dollar to the man in the township.

The chairman said one-fourth of the citizens will need to buy bread, and will not have money to do it with.

The secretary confirmed this statement, and thought that many will not only suffer, but will perish unless they are helped.

Mr. Burnett, farmer, corroborated the above as applied to his district; said one-sixth of the population, to his knowledge, will suffer, unless relieved from abroad.

Sheriff Moore, of Freedom township, said the corn crop is almost a failure. The crops generally in the county are a failure. Corn on the bottom lands will not yield five bushels to the acre.

W. Deeds, farmer, of Timberhill, has forty acres of corn, which is said to be the best in the county, and will not average eight bushels to the acre, and wormy at that.

John Janeway, farmer, of Mill Creek, Marmaton township, says the corn on Mill creek is much worm-eaten. Wheat, oats, Hungarian grass, and vegetables, are all a failure. Many are leaving the county; many more have neither bread nor the means to get it.

The above facts are corroborated by the statement of Dr. Norman T. Winans, of Bourbon county, near the Allen county line, who says that in a tract of land in Allen county, embracing about nine hundred persons, where twenty-five hundred acres are under cultivation, there are not two hundred and twenty-five bushels of old corn for seed and subsistence; that the present crop will not yield two bushels to the acre, and even *that* is being eaten by the worms. The people have exhausted their all in improvements, and have not the means to live, and will lose their claims if offered for sale. Many have left; more would have gone, but lack the means. Valuable claims are already abandoned. This portion of the country has been settled within the last eighteen months. To his knowledge, within eight weeks one hundred and sixty persons have left the county.

J. C. Burnett, W. R. Griffith, and Sheriff Moore were appointed a committee to furnish a statement and open a correspondence with Thaddeus Hyatt, of New York, to obtain relief.

The census report, it is thought, will give to Bourbon county four thousand inhabitants.

WAUBUNSEE COUNTY.

HARVEY'S SETTLEMENT, *September* 11, 1860.

Editors State Record: Will you please publish the following statement of facts, reported at an adjourned meeting of
the citizens of this neighborhood, and unanimously adopted?

J. F. BALLARD, Secretary.

To our fellow-citizens of the neighboring States, greeting:

Whereas, various rumors have gone forth with respect to
the existing state of things in connection with the unprecedented drought now prevailing over our own and the section
of the country surrounding us, we have deemed it a duty we
owe ourselves, our families, and others, to make known to
you our situation with reference thereto, by a plain statement
of facts.

Although we have had occasional showers, there have
been but three or four sufficient to moisten the ground to a
greater depth than two inches since the memorable storm of
the 19th June, 1859. During the summer and the latter part
of the spring, the ground has been perfectly dry at a depth
of three or four inches. How far downwards has not been
ascertained—the fact that many forest trees are withering
and dying, is suggestive.

In consequence of the small supply of rain, unprecedented,
probably, in the history of our common country, our crops
are a total failure; our wells and springs are dried up, and
the water in our creeks fast receding and disappearing.

At the present time, the little corn that has grown, is being
cut for fodder. In a few days not a stalk will be standing
in our fields worth the expense of cutting it down. We shall
not have an ear of corn for seed.

No spring wheat was sown, and the little that was sown
in the fall withered and died as the moisture, induced by
the light snows and frosts of winter, receded.

In our gardens the effects of the drought have been fatal. We may say, nothing, absolutely nothing, has gladdened our eyes, or gratified the palate from them. Our peas did not even blossom. Although tomatoes, cabbages, and other vegetables were watered by our own hands with assiduity and care, our labor has been entirely lost.

A few weeks ago we sowed buckwheat. A few light showers which fell soon afterward, revived our hopes, and we flattered ourselves that that labor had not been in vain. But the same causes which militated against us in our other labors, have prevailed against us in this.

We had hoped, too, that a favorable season might favor our crop of potatoes, a much larger breadth of ground having been appropriated for that purpose than heretofore. But that resource has failed us; everything has failed us but the determination to make the very best we can of the future. What that has in store for us, is known only to Him who " tempers the winds to the shorn lamb."

It is needless for us to appeal to you for help in this time of famine. We believe a knowledge of our actual necessities will be sufficient to induce those who have " enough and to spare," the magnanimous and liberal of more favored parts of the country, to help us in this, our time of need.

We have been induced to take these steps by the assurance that many of you have expressed a willingness and desire to furnish those who, by the famine here, have been deprived of the ordinary resources for obtaining the staff of life with the means of subsistence, until we can again cultivate our fields and obtain sustenance therefrom.

We will cheerfully submit to any self-denial here, rather than leave our homes to become strangers elsewhere.

Some are already leaving, but the most of us, if we desired to do so, cannot. Those conversant with life in a new country, need not be reminded of the reason of this. We must stay and abide the consequences.

ALLEN HODGSON, President.

T F. BALLARD, *Secretary.*

The above is from the Topeka State Record, and fully confirms all the other testimony.

OSAGE COUNTY.

The condition of this county is very forcibly set forth in the following letter, written to the Lawrence Republican by O. H. Sheldon:

SUPERIOR, *August* 21, 1860.

EDITOR REPUBLICAN: As you have solicited communications from the farmers concerning their prospects as to crops, I will say that in this county, not one hundred bushels of grain has been or will be harvested, excepting corn; and even corn will not bear more than one-eighth of an average yield. A large portion of the fields will not even produce roasting-ears. I have under cultivation about sixty acres, but shall not have over one hundred bushels on the whole. Our potato crop, without doubt, is an entire failure. To my knowledge, but two persons in the county have old corn for sale. One of them refuses to sell, only for family use, which is much better than to sell for feed to stock. I hope others will follow his example. We shall need all the corn to "keep the breath of life in us" during the next year.

Grass is very light in this portion of the county; south of here, on that portion of the Sac and Fox reserve lately treated for, it is more plenty. Those having claims are making preparations for putting up a large quantity for sale. Would it not be better for them to winter stock on shares.? If they will not, much of the stock will die, as but few are able to buy hay.

There will be much suffering here this winter for the want of food and clothing. Many have struggled for the last five years through all the troubles and trials incident to a pioneer's life, expecting to realize the pleasures of a comfortable home; but alas! how sadly they are disappointed; their hopes are forever blasted—their money is gone, their health ruined; they have not funds to return to their friends; and, worse than all, their farms which they have prized so highly are soon to fall into the hands of the speculator.

What is to be done for the afflicted I hardly know. I have but little faith in sending agents East, for they will want, and will take, nearly all they receive for their time and trouble. Nearly all the goods that were sent to this settlement for the poor, were sold to the highest bidder, cash down. So the poorest got nothing.

One half of the mortgages on our lands are held by Lecompton Democrats, who have no sympathy for "Black Republicans;" and they are ready and willing to take our lands as soon as the law will allow them. If Eastern capitalists can be induced to lend us money, at ten per cent. per annum interest, to take up our old mortgages with, we might get through; if not, we must struggle on and abide the consequences.

The drought of this season may give Kansas a hard name, but it should not. It is the first one of the kind that has ever happened with us, while it is quite common in the States It has convinced me that our soil is better than all other soils in standing the drought. With a drought of half the duration in the East, nothing would have grown. It is strange that we even have pastures for our stock.

To those who think of leaving the Territory, let me say that produce will be high next year, and if they can stay to raise another crop, it is their interest to do so. Times are easier East, and if our friends will only help us until we can help ourselves, they will save from an inevitable calamity many of the poor pioneers who have suffered long in Kansas.

O. H. S.

COFFEE COUNTY.

THE LEROY MEETING.

At a meeting held at Leroy, Coffee county, September 5, 1860, Rev. B. Wheat, chairman:

Dr. Butler stated that many cattle have died of the Texas

fever on the route of the droves from Texas. No wheat has been raised, and there is but little old corn in the county.

Elisha Amesdale, miller, said there is not old corn enough to do the people for more than two months, if used to feed hogs or any other purpose than bread. There is not one fourth the fall wheat that should be for seed. It is two dollars per bushel, and money so scarce that the people cannot buy it; there are not over two hundred and fifty bushels, and that of an inferior quality.

Mr. Johnson, merchant, says the wheat in the country is of very poor quality, and the corn will not average five bushels to the acre.

Hiram McMahon says, the average will not be five bushels to the acre, and very wormy. One third of the people in the neighborhood have left; there will not be corn fodder enough for the cattle.

Alexander Hamilton, farmer, says the corn will not average two bushels to the acre. He has been over the whole country. Eighty acres of corn that he planted this year will not yield one bushel to the acre. All the corn is much damaged by the worm. There are not five thousand bushels of old corn in the whole county. If people should use corn as they did last year, he is confident that it would not last two weeks. The cattle are dying, and their disease is contagious. There are no potatoes; if rain should come in a few days there may be a few turnips; [none came.] From lands of which he raised sixty bushels to the acre last year, he has no corn this year to feed his hogs. His hogs he was willing to give away to the destitute, but he would not sell them to speculators.

Elder Wheat (Methodist) was of the opinion that the destitution was not exaggerated; there was no alternative but great suffering or relief. The only green thing that he had been able to raise was three cucumbers, and he had planted in garden produce, &c., thirty acres. Did not want, himself, but felt for others, whom he was unable to relieve—and they were so numerous he had little hope of any effectual relief at all adequate to their necessity. The people were industrious, but their crops were all failures, and they could only look to God and their friends. Mr. Hyatt received his thanks for his disinterested benevolence, and through him he would appeal for further aid.

Elder Phillips (Christian preacher) said he had traveled twenty-five or thirty miles to-day to look for grass, but found none. He confirmed the statements of Elder Wheat, and thought Kansas better adapted to stand drought than any of the States.

D. K. Debble, farmer, said he planted thirty acres of corn; will get about fifty bushels. Sowed twenty acres of field wheat; got nothing. Of twenty-five acres of spring wheat, got fifteen bushels. Cutting fodder, it will require one day to cut enough for eight head of cattle for two days. More than half the people had to borrow money to pre-empt their lands, and many others made great sacrifices. He complained of the hardship of having to pay for their lands.

Much other testimony was given, but all confirming the above.

W. A. Jenkins and Elder B. Wheat were appointed a committee to correspond with Mr. Hyatt for relief.

THE BURLINGTON MEETING.

At a meeting held at Burlington, Coffee county, September 6, 1860, Colonel Leonard chairman, B. A. Kingsberry secretary—

Mr. Ebenezer Hooper, of Leroy, farmer, said he had sowed eighty acres of wheat, and planted thirty of corn; the chinch-bug killed the wheat, the drought and the worm destroyed the corn. He also planted potatoes, which would not produce anything. There are many persons in this township in a similar situation. A great majority of the people in this county will be destitute of seed next spring. Many families are leaving to avoid starvation.

Clark Fritt, farmer, Neosho township, has thirty-two acres broken—old ground; plowed three times and hoed it three times, and does not believe there is five bushels of corn fit for bread. He had lost six head of cattle of the Spanish fever; forty hogs must die, as he has no corn to feed them. There are not a hundred and fifty bushels of old corn in the township; not wheat enough for seed. His land last year produced fifty bushels corn to the acre. Nine families had left his neighborhood, and many more would leave if they had the means. David Manly started with his family of six children, with but $1.50, thirty pounds of flour and a little meal. Mr. Woodworth left with his family and team, having no provisions.

G. N. Simms, Avon township, says he has forty acres under cultivation, which was broken four years ago; he planted in April and May, and has no corn at all; averaged forty bushels to the acre last year. He sowed wheat last fall and this spring, but realized only two bushels and a half, and unfit for seed at that. One acre of navy beans never blossomed. He will only have a few sweet potatoes, and one-third of a crop of sorghum; of seven acres of buckwheat, nothing.

James A. Grimes of Avon, has about thirty bushels of old corn to bread him.

W. Watrous, of Avon, said that for six miles on Lost creek there is not over a hundred and fifty bushels of old corn.

William A. Ela, of Hampden, says he has one hundred acres in corn; will have five bushels to the acre of "*corn and worms;*" has not found an ear without the worm in it. Has travelled through the county, and, bad as Coffee county is, it is better off than many others, especially in the northern part. Such a drought as they had in Kansas would have killed even the trees in Massachusetts.

John T. Cox, Ottumwa township, says: In our township
4

the early corn has suffered much. There are about four hundred bushels of old corn in the whole township; no money. The people being compelled to pay for their lands many have left the neighborhood.

Wm. Martindale, Ottumwa township, says, wheat crops last year and year before averaged forty bushels, and weighed sixty-two pounds to the bushel; but we have no crop this year; he might get five bushels to the acre on forty acres.

Thomas Arnold, Burlington township, says that he has raised, before this year, one hundred bushels to the acre; he will not this year average eight bushels to the acre; two acres of potatoes will produce nothing; buckwheat has wholly failed, and there are not twenty-five bushels of old corn in his neighborhood.

Gen. Whistler, Burlington, says he has heretofore averaged fifty bushels of corn to the acre; this year he may get ten bushels from fifty acres, and has worked it better than usual. He has known Kansas fifteen years, and never knew anything like this drought; usually, with good cultivation, the Neosho bottoms will produce one hundred bushels to the acre. There is not sufficient old corn to keep the people of the county; a great many persons are leaving the country for want of the necessaries of life.

Township committees were appointed to make further investigations, and report to Thaddeus Hyatt, with a view to some relief for the people.

NOTE.—It will be observed above that Mr. Cox reports *four hundred* bushels of old corn in his township of Ottumwa. A reference to his subsequent report, [see the Ottumwa meeting below,] *after* a rigid investigation, shows but *one hundred and thirty-nine*, a worse condition than had been supposed. This has been the result of thorough investigation everywhere, as appears throughout the testimony.

THE OTTUMWA MEETING.

A meeting was held at Ottumwa, Coffee county, September 6, 1860, John T. Cox chairman, W. F. Mills secretary—

Jesse Kennedy of California township, said he had sixty acres in corn, which will not average ten bushels to the acre. Last year he raised forty. Wheat, oats, and potatoes had all failed in the county. There is a little old corn in the county, which might do some service if divided. Money is very scarce; the people had borrowed money on their lands, and will now loose their claims.

Mr. D. A. Hawkins believed Kansas a better country to stand drought than Kentucky, but this year it has been fatal. Of twenty-five acres only will he hope for half a crop of corn. Potatoes had failed entire. Many of his neighbors' crops are not so good as his. Some will find it very hard to get through the winter.

William Brewer, of California township, said his wheat and oats both failed, and buckwheat is not good; the prospect for crops in the whole country is very slim; it will be a tight rub to feed the people, and but little for stock.

John M. Singer, California township, says he has got ninety acres, twenty of which will not produce anything, while a portion will yield, at most, fifteen bushels to the acre; all other crops have failed. There will not be corn enough to do the neighborhood, and many must suffer; last year he averaged forty bushels to the acre; there is no grass of any kind that will pay for cutting, and there is no corn for sale.

Jacob Hoover, California township, says, last year his wheat yielded forty bushels to the acre, this year he may get twenty; there is no country where corn can better stand the drought.

Much other testimony was given; after which a committee was appointed to make further investigation, and to report to Thaddeus Hyatt. The committee completed their labors, and sent their report to Mr. Hyatt, at Atchison, which exhibits the following, viz:

Wants of Ottumwa township, as condensed from the report of John T. Cox, Esq., made September 15, 1860:

Whole number of families in township	66
Whole number of persons in township	344
Land paid for—acres	4,180
Land not paid for—acres	7,020
Land planted in corn last season	862½
Probable yield in bushels	5,366
Bushels of old corn on hand	139
Acres of buckwheat sown this season	77
Probable yield in bushels	40
Acres of wheat sown this season	77
Amount of yield in bushels	16
Amount of potatoes planted this season	7¾
Number of head of horses to winter	448
Number of hogs—one third to fatten	688
Acres of garden this season	12⅓
Value of garden stuff—mostly consumed	$87
Amount of cash on hand	70 80
Amount of seed wheat wanted in bushels	315
Amount of seed corn wanted	190

(A greater amount of corn for seed will be required, as that raised will not be fit for seed.)

Amount of seed potatoes wanted in bushels	160
Number of families without money	54
Number of families without any supply for the coming winter	48
Number of families with half a supply	8
Number of families supplied	10

There are, in addition this, some twenty young men, who have raised no produce, but paid their way by labor.

The report from California township is very similar, and quite as bad as Ottumwa.

Note. The condition of this township presents the most favorable aspect of any township I found in all my travels, it having been blessed with a fall of about six inches of rain.

MISCELLANEOUS TESTIMONY,

AS NOTED IN

𝔇iary of 𝔗wenty-five 𝔇ays 𝔍ourneyings

THROUGH THE FAMINE LAND,

FROM AUGUST 22, TO SEPTEMBER 15, WITH EXTRACTS FROM LETTERS.

BUTLER, HUNTER, GREENWOOD, MADISON, AND OTTOE COUNTIES.

Mr. J. C. Lambdin, in a letter to Judge Arny, from Chelsea, Butler county, September 20, 1860, says that he has visited and heard from many families in these counties whose destitute condition is truly alarming. Mr. Lambdin continues :

"As to crops in these counties, there are none; they are a complete failure. There will not be twenty bushels of corn raised in Butler, Hunter, and Ottoe counties, and not exceeding that amount of wheat; no potatoes; the buckwheat crop is entirely destroyed by grasshoppers. In Butler county there are about six hundred inhabitants; in Hunter one hundred, and in Ottoe one hundred and fifty, and at least three-fourths of that number are almost destitute of money, clothing, and provisions. Very few have more stock than can supply their immediate wants. Some, indeed, have been deprived of their last cow by a disease that has prevailed in this country to some extent, called Spanish fever. I found many families that had not more than one bushel of corn meal in the house; that, with some buffalo meat, and the milk they get, composes their daily food. The people are in a wretched condition, and unless supplies are furnished from some source, much suffering will be the result. Most of the settlers have been here over two years; their means are exhausted; they have nothing. I have travelled several hundred miles in Southern Kansas, and this state of things does not only exist in these counties, but, according to my observation, in all Kansas south of the Kaw river."

Judge Lambdin is senator elect under the Wyandotte constitution.

There are six or eight families (in Ottoe county) of colored persons, who have been driven from Arkansas by the law compelling "free negroes" to leave the State. They are represented as industrious, but now in want, owing to the present drought.

H. T. Hunter, of Madison county, states that he has eight acres of corn, which he thinks may yield fifteen bushels to the acre, but very wormy. Wheat through his section is an entire failure. There is but little old corn in his township. On the Verdigris, the crops are almost an entire failure. Mr. B. F. Vanhorn has a large field of corn which he has offered to sell for twenty-five cents per acre. There is not corn enough in the county to do the people. Population on the creeks, about five hundred; represents their condition as deplorable. Many have borrowed money to pre-empt, and have mortgaged their claims.

Myrock Huntley, of same county, from four hundred acres planted, will realize nothing but fodder. Corn is a legal tender. A few will have bread and water. Many are going away. Bread and groceries are needed.

Judge Graham, of the same county, states that the corn crop in his neighborhood may yield ten bushels to the acre, but very wormy. Very little old corn in the county; only ten bushels in the mill. If it does not rain in a week [it did not] there will be no potatoes. The population of the county cannot be sustained by the present crop. Fifty-three head of cattle died in a week.

Thomas A. Hill of Greenwood county says there will not be a bushel of corn to the acre in Greenwood county. Eighty or ninety families have already left, and others would go if able.

Mosely, the celebrated buffalo hunter, reports that the waters have ceased to run in the big bend of the Big Arkansas. He has formerly lived on the Little Arkansas, where the destitution became so great, that to the extent of fifteen miles square not a white settler remains, and the only inhabitant who has not deserted is "Buckner," the negro. Mosely, to better his condition, changed to Greenwood county, where he is now staying. He says there is, even there, not a bushel of corn, as he believes, in the whole county. They have no groceries; no money. The people have lost even the seed they planted; for meat, they are depending upon the buffalo; and to purchase bread, having no money, they depend upon wolf skins, the legal tender of the country. "Wolf skin," remarked Mosely, quaintly, *"wolf skin is lawful tender here; and you've got first to catch him, at that!"*

John L. Pratt, of Chelsea, Butler county, says there are no crops in his county — not a cucumber even. No old corn in the county; not much money; and what wheat could be raised has been used for pre-emption of land. Many persons were compelled to mortgage their claims, and others gave up entirely and left the country. There is *not a dollar in money* to the man. Fifteen townships of land were offered for sale at Fort Scott on the 13th of August, and the people were compelled to go about one hundred and fifty miles to pre-empt their lands. Buffalo meat is a legal tender. There is not a grain of old corn on hand on Walnut creek — an extent of sixty-five miles—except what has been hauled from Cottonwood, a distance of fifty miles. The grasshoppers came to that country in a cloud about two weeks ago, and after destroying the corn and the buckwheat, are now eating the leaves of the trees. He saw clouds of them in the sky; at that time they came from the northwest.

Aug. 24.—Met Peter Welsh, from the neighborhood of Fort Scott, in the Osage country, who testified as follows: Has lived thirty years in this country, and never saw anything like this; has to haul provisions for his family one hundred and fifty miles. The Osage Indians have gone to the Buffalo country to keep from starving. Chetopee, the chief, 93 years old, never knew till this year a want of grass for the ponies to live on, and corn has always been raised till this year. Unless there is some help for southern and western Kansas, it will be depopulated; homes are vacated; people are moving out; women have been compelled to cut squashes with the bloom on to cook for their children.

Met five wagons and twenty-four persons from Walnut creek, Butler county. William Sherman said he had a good place and was well fixed, but could not stay and starve. The people are now living on corn bread and corn coffee. Last spring he was offered seven hundred dollars for his improvements; in order to leave the country, he now sold them for a yoke of cattle and a wagon not worth one hundred dollars. The people have stayed till they have worn out all their clothes, and, having nothing to eat, must leave or starve.

EXTRACTS FROM LETTERS.

A very intelligent man, in behalf of himself and another sufferer, writes from Owl creek, Woodson county, under date of September 14, as follows:

"DEAR SIR: Men under some circumstances, become desperate. * * Men of sensitive feelings would scarcely appeal to strangers until the last resort—until hope had well nigh fled. We are bold, but it is the boldness that desperation gives. * * * We ask of you a little money *to buy bread.*

You have seen our faces. * * * We must have aid from some source. We have raised no crop; we have no team; not a dollar in money — how can we get away? S. N. H. lost well nigh all by fire. I have lost more than all! She who was the life, the light, the joy and pride of my home; who never murmured; who always welcomed me; the mother of my children; — she now lies within the clay, sleeps her long death-sleep now beneath this Kansas soil! Do not repulse us; do not slight our request. We ask not for ourselves, but for our hungry, ragged, motherless, destitute children! We do not wish to *beg;* we ask it as a *loan,* not as a pure *gift;* we are willing to work. Can you aid us? Will you?   E. C.

"P. S. No rain yet. Indeed, rain would do but little good: *vegetation is dead!* A general exodus seems about to take place. Whole neighborhoods — without exaggeration, *whole neighborhoods* are being deserted!   E. C.

"N. B. The utterly *helpless* and the utterly *hoggish* alone remain!   E. C."

The allusion in the above letter, "You have seen our faces," refers to the fact that I had met and conversed with both these gentlemen about ten days previous. The condition of Woodson county, as above depicted, is affirmed by the assessor of the county.

Mr. Condict, having visited every cabin in the county, and seen all the people, represents an entire destitution, such as prevails in nearly every county of the Territory. He states that the amount of money in Woodson county, as verified under oath, would not exceed *one dollar per man!*

The Rev. T. P. Killen, in a letter written from Carlyle, Allen county, under date of September 19, 1860, and addressed to me at Atchison, says:

"We are truly in the deep waters, and I fear many must suffer. We will labor for the best, but I must confess we are at a loss to know how to advise our people. In the midst of our troubles to know what we shall eat and drink, *the official news of our land sales* on the 3d December, COMES DOWN UPON US LIKE A THUNDERBOLT! What shall we do? Will our friends in the East answer the question? * * *

Hoping we will hear from you, and feeling confident that the great and good who have plenty will not close their ears to the cries of the suffering, I remain,

Yours, &c.,   J. P. KILLEN."

STORY OF A POOR FAMILY.

The following story is from my diary of September 9th. The simple, touching narrative of this poor family is but a picture of thousands, and shows the practical working and cruelty of the land sales. The condition of this family was brought to my notice by an old man named Bryant, who had come over to the Emporia meeting of September 8th, and called on me at the hotel in order to tell me what he knew of the distress in his neighborhood.

"There's a family near me, named Adams," said Bryant; "a father, mother, and seven children; but the eldest is away from home—jest as good people as any on us; and they hevn't a mouthful to eat but what the neighbors gin 'em I've kind o' kept the critters along as well as I could, but I can't *dew* it much longer; we're on our last bag of flour ourselves, and not a dollar in the world to get more. Why, sir, people at the East don't know nothin about our situation! they hevn't any *idee* on it!" and the old man detailed to me his own history. His speech, his looks, his earnestness, his active movements, and everything about him showed him to be one of those industrious and thriving men from New England, whose hands are never idle for want of something to do. But the trouble, as Bryant represented it, was that when he had got his job of blacksmithing done for a neighbor, the poor neighbor had no means of paying him!—neither money nor provisions! Continuing his story of the poor family, he remarked: "What on airth the poor woman and her children are *to dew* I don't know. I don't see but they *must* starve! Looks like it." And every muscle of the old man's honest countenance expressed more forcibly than his earnest words how deeply he felt for them.

HOW I FOUND THE FAMILY.

They were living in a little "shake house," a few miles from Emporia, in which they had passed the whole of last winter. On entering the cabin, its poverty was at once apparent.

Two poor looking beds, an apology for a table, no chairs, a miscellaneous trunk, and a broken box which answered for a seat, constituted the household furniture entire. A yoke of oxen, nine fowls, and three young pigs inventoried the wealth of the family. A woman, whose face had evidently known more beauty and less sorrow, responded to my questions. Anxiety, suffering, and want were now plainly written upon her countenance. "Rather poor looking walls madam," I remarked to her, "to keep out a winter's wind." "Yes, sir," she replied, "we find it pretty cold; I pasted paper over all the cracks, as well as I could, but the March winds blew them off; we had a cold time of it; but we got through." "Your house, madam, has not the appearance of very great abundance; how are you provided for? How much flour have you?" "Not any, sir." "What groceries?" "None!" "No tea?" "No, sir." "Nor coffee nor sugar?" "None, sir!" "What have you?" "*About a peck of meal.*"

"When this is gone, what then?" A shade of anxiety passed over the poor woman's face as she looked at her children, and I could see that she struggled with her feelings. "Well, sir, I don't know." "Have you no means of getting anything? Neither money nor work?" "As to money, sir, my husband may possibly have *fifty cents*, but not to exceed this, and this is all the money we have. As to work, there is none to be had; I have helped along by making baskets;" and here she stooped down and brought out a few willow baskets from under the bed, apologizing at the same time, for the character of her storehouse; "these, sir, are such as I make and used to sell; but now, no one wants to buy; it seems like as though no one had any money."

" Where is your husband? "   " He is over at his *landlord's*
doing a small job of work to *pay the rent* of this house! "
" Then you hire? "   " We are compelled to; we have NO
HOME NOW! "   " Had you one? "   " Yes, sir, my husband
took a very fine claim, and put up a cabin, which we lived
in for nearly a year, but THE LAND SALES CAME, and *we
could not pay for the land;* my husband knew he could not
pay *four per cent. a month* for money, and so we had to give it
up! and now, sir, we are without any home of our own! "

From the Washington Intelligencer, July 31, 1860.

THE DROUGHT IN THE SOUTHWEST.—The St. Louis Evening News of the 25th instant gives some gloomy accounts
of the general and disastrous drought that has prevailed over
the whole South and blasted the hopes of the planting region
in their corn crops.   The News says:
* * * "The southwest portion of our own State is also
visited, and we have a letter giving a most melancholy account of the blasted cornfields in the counties of Benton,
Polk, St. Clair, Bates, Henry, Hickory, and other counties."
[These counties border on Southern Kansas.]

BLACK-JACK, *Douglas county, Sept.* 23, 1860.

DEAR SIR: Necessity has compelled me to appeal to you
for relief. I would state I have lived here near four years,
and have had a series of bad luck ever since I have been
here. I first settled on Indian land; I did not discover it
for nearly a whole year; I lost all that year's labor. I
moved out on the prairie, and commenced again to open
another farm; that year I was sick with the typhoid fever.
Last year was the first year that I was prospering, but my
means being exhausted I could not make much headway,
but calculated that this present year would make all right

with us. But alas! we are mistaken again. My crop is all gone; I have not been able to get any seed from corn, potatoes, or buckwheat, and all garden truck is failed. The Spanish fever has got in among our cattle. I lost two last week— one a very fine milch cow, the only cow we had. I have used up most of my grain sacks, to make dresses for my daughters to hide their nakedness. Our diet is composed of corn meal and water, and it is most all gone. I have been sick with the fever the last two weeks, and am not able to do a day's work, if there was work to be had.

This is the condition I am placed in at the approach of winter—no work; not able to work if I had any; nothing to sell, to procure food and clothing; no crop; with a family of a wife and seven children, the oldest twelve years, the youngest three months. I, therefore, in behalf of my family, appeal to you for relief.

Hoping you will give this a favorable consideration, I remain your humble servant,

C. B. RICE.

To Hon. M. F. CONWAY.

I also submit the following Appeal of the Highland Presbytery of Kansas Territory.

The Presbytery at Highland, in session at Wyandotte City, Kansas, desire to make known to the Church and friends abroad, as nearly as they can, the wants and destitutions of our Territory, consequent upon the drought of the past year.

Since Kansas has been known by red or white man, she has not before, so far as is known, failed to produce abundantly from her rich soil, and to repay largely and bountifully the labors of the husbandman. This year it has not been so. The rains have been withheld, crops have failed, and great destitution prevails in parts of our Territory.

We see, and we recognize the hand of God in this. We

see his footsteps, we hear his voice, and we would "be still and know that he is God."

With painful interest have we listened to the statements made by brethren coming up from all parts of the Territory, and we trust that we have now the facts that will enable us to make some correct, though very general and very brief statements in the case.

The counties bordering on the Missouri, and some districts along the Kansas river and larger streams, are not in a suffering condition. In most of these districts a half crop has been raised, and from some of them something can be spared to help the more destitute.

In the south and west, and on the high prairie lands, crops have been, in most cases, entire failures. Nor has it been for want of labor and effort on the part of farmers. Early in the spring, large fields of spring wheat were sown. This failing, the ground was ploughed over and planted in corn; this again failing, the ground was sown in turnips or buckwheat; and this also proved a failure. Many have really nothing. Most persons have come to the Territory with small means, spent what they had in improving and in living, depending on an expected crop to meet the wants of the future.

There is also an alarming destitution of clothing. Wool and flax are but little raised here, and not yet manufactured; and men have been depending upon the crops to procure these from abroad. Winter is near, and large families may be found where there is not a shoe, and scarcely a comfortable woolen garment for the winter. In this state of things, Presbytery deem it a duty to publish the facts, and address them mainly to our own church and people in the States. So far as our own church and people are concerned in Kansas near one-half of them do not stand in need of any help from abroad. The Churches of Carlisle, Wyandotte, Leavenworth, Atchison, Highland, Iowa Point and Lecompton, and Lawrence in part, are provided, and some of them can spare something for others. The remainder of our Churches, containing a membership of about two hundred and fifty, and a connection with perhaps two or three thousand persons, do stand greatly in need. Other parties of large means* have, as we understand, in view plans to meet, to some extent, the wants of the Territory, and it seemed proper in us to make a special effort, mainly in behalf of our own people. * *

We only ask of those who have received largely of God's bounties, that they divide us a small portion. And especially do we desire that your earnest prayers may accompany your gifts, that these chastisements, which "for the present may seem grievous, may work in us the peaceable fruits of rightousness."

J. S. REASOR, *Moderator.*
S. M. IRVIN, *Stated Clerk.*

---

* "*Other parties of large means.*"—My twenty-five days tour, of nearly a thousand miles travel, through the Territory, awakened a wide-spread hope and a general expectation that speedy relief would in some way follow my investigations. I judge that the remark above, "*other parties of large means,*" &c., refers to those expectations. Had the New York Tribune been as true to the Kansas of 1860 as it seemed to be to the Kansas of 1856, this reasonable expectation of a starving people would have been realized. But my letters to that journal, dated from and written in the famine-land, and appealing for the sufferers, were *suppressed!* and to this hour its columns that know so well how to thunder, and that might have saved, have remained as cold and dead as the speechless, and livid lips of the starved mothers and perishing babes whom it heartlessly abandons in this their mortal hour of extremity, of agony, and of despair. Had it bestowed upon these poor people even one-half the attention it gives to a "Heenan and Sayers" prize fight, hundreds might have been saved, who must now inevitably perish before assistance can reach them.

The following I clip from the Philadelphia "Press" of the 27th instant. How painfully it confirms all that I have stated above! Alas! hour by hour the accumulating facts become more and more terrible.

"*The Great Kansas Famine — Extreme Suffering among the Inhabitants — 30,000 People Wanting Food.*

"The Chicago Press and Tribune says: The facts cannot

longer escape the attention of the most tardy and incredulous, that an extraordinary condition of affairs prevails throughout a large share of the new Territory of Kansas, where there is at present 'a famine in the land,' so general, so inclusive, reached by such stages and falling upon a community so situated, that it is doubtful whether it has had any parallel within the present century. The thrilling descriptions that reach us from various and reliable sources, painfully realize the most vivid and painful narratives of such visitations, in Scripture, which we have been to apt to deem well nigh impossible to our age of civilization, and certainly among our own citizens, on our own soil. Even the great famine in Ireland, historic in the tales of suffering and lists of generous deeds, whose memory will live in the plaintive

"' Give me three grains of corn, mother,'

seems to promise to be unsurpassed in the scattered homes of a new Territory, unless help speedily reaches them, for thousands now suffering for food, to whom November, now at hand, will usher in fresh terrors."

By and by, when the ears of the country shall tingle with tales of the dreadful sufferings of our poor Kansas population, and when the heart of the country shall grow sick with the horrors that will then be hourly accumulating upon it, the question will be asked in a thousand quarters, Why were not these things foreseen in time to avert and to save? And my reply to the country in that hour will be as it now is: *They were foreseen!* and they might have been averted! and they would have been, had the New York Tribune done its duty.

I wrote with warmth and with feeling indeed, for who could help it under the circumstances? Take one instance or two. As I was writing in my room at Atchison one evening, a friend came in, remarking, with much feeling: "Hyatt, I begin to say as you did yesterday, 'I would not stay sixty days longer in this place, empty handed, to inherit a life to come!' A poor fellow met me in the street just now, and looking me full in the face, says: 'I've got to break into some store to-night! my family have'nt a mouthful of food, and I can't let them starve!'" And my friend continuing, said: "Hyatt, I am growing sicker and sicker every hour." And then he told me of a poor man who had walked ninety miles from the back country to reach Atchison, begging a night's lodging and a meal's victuals on the way ; got a few dollars together at Atchison by a few days work ; purchased provisions with it for his starving family and then, with the provisions on his back, *walked* ninety miles to save them from perishing!

Another case that he brought to my notice was that of a poor family at Winthrop, opposite Atchison: *two dead children* in the cabin, another sick, and the father and mother both down with fever at the same time! This, not as the direct consequences of starving, but resultant effects from hardships and want, following loss of crops!

I may as well say, right here, that the friend alluded to above is General S. C. Pomeroy, of Atchison, who, with Judge Arny, of Hyatt, accompanied me through the whole tour. These friends are generously devoting all their time and energies now to the suffering: the former at Atchison receives and forwards to the needy whatever aid my friend Arny may succeed in getting at the West, or I may possibly secure by personal exertions at the East.

5

CONCLUDING APPEAL.

I think your Excellency will not regard as out of place an explanatory word here touching the origin of this present movement of the undersigned in behalf of Kansas. My connection with Kansas affairs in 1856, (which was purely moral,) had given me too clear an insight into the condition of that noble and brave, but unfortunate people, to permit any apathy on my part under so burning an appeal as is contained in the following:

From the Washington Intelligencer, August 6, 1860.

THE DROUGHT IN KANSAS.—We have had frequent reports within a few months of the terrible drought prevailing in the Territory of Kansas, more particularly in the southern section. For nearly or quite a year there has but little rain fallen in the Territory, and in southern Kansas it is stated that not more than four or five inches of rain have fallen during the year. The consequence is there will be no crop, and how the people of that unfortunate section of country are to be fed during the coming winter becomes a question of the gravest importance. A letter from Mound City, dated July 7th, published in the New York Tribune, says: "Our corn is near or quite dead; our grass for hay is entirely out of the question, for there is none; the hot sun has entirely destroyed it." The letter speaks almost bitterly of the impending ruin staring the people in the face. It says: "Hear me tell God's truth. As I write in my house the wind flaps over me; the sun heats it so that the wind almost burns me; my wife is now roasting eggs on the stone steps in front of my house; the stove and tin boiler are too hot to bear my hands on them, standing in the house where the sun cannot touch them; they are hot by the wind blowing on them through the open door. Why, every flap of the wind is like the heat of fire from a burning building. I have just shut the door to keep the hot wind from blowing on me, so that I can write. To say that it has not rained for twelve months would not be telling the truth; but to say that not more than four or five inches of rain had fallen in that time would be nearly or quite true. Now, for God's sake, what are the people to do? We can't stay here without food for ourselves or cattle."

The letter here quoted was written by Mr. Stillwell, who lives on Mine Creek, in Linn county, and whom, when there in August, I saw and conversed with. The fearful picture drawn by this gentleman in the above, is fully confirmed by the reports embraced in Professor Henry's letter, as well as by testimony at the Mound City meeting herein above recorded. I read Mr. Stillwell's letter as soon as published; my heart burned. He alluded to the help once vouchsafed to famine-stricken Ireland, and asked imploringly if some "good Samaritan from the East" would not have compassion on the perishing people of Kansas. I looked for some one to start — but none went: so leaving all, I said I must go. Though I have not means sufficient to relieve so wide-spread a calamity, I will at least explore and report. The country cannot fail to listen: the heart of the country will surely respond. I did not doubt that the *press* of the country would heartily co-operate. I went to Kansas. I traversed its burnt-up prairies; I crossed its dried-up streams; I saw where great rivers had shrunk to stagnant pools; I saw expiring fishes in the shallow waters, par-boiling under the scorching heavens; I felt the hot breath of the siroccos; I cooled my temples with wet compresses, as day after day I rode through the flooding heats of the glaring sun. The people gathered; they saw hope in the fact that the country was to be appealed to; they took courage; some who were preparing to leave, reconsidered and remained, believing now that help would surely come. I traveled by day and wrote letters by night. I mailed the letters to the New York Tribune, thinking thus to introduce to the press generally, and through them to the country, a knowledge of the fearful things I had been eye-witness to.

I was ill when I started, but worse when I returned, for the

press of the country was silent! Only *one* of my letters had
been permitted to see the light! My "Appeal" was entirely
suppressed. As its style did not differ materially from many
I had written in 1856, this certainly could not have caused
its suppression. From Atchison (to which place I returned
again from the tour) I sent telegram after telegram to New
York to know why Kansas received no attention. Having
myself in 1856 acted in good faith for a suffering people, I
had never credited the partizan charges of a contrary nature
against a rival party. I had regarded the party advantages
and disadvantages of that struggle as mere incidents; and I
had gone into it, as I would to-day enlist under Garibaldi,
purely in behalf of liberty, striking only for great principles;
for humanity only; not for party. Naturally enough, then,
I looked for the same co-operation and for the same earnestness, and to the same quarters. I beg your Excellency to
contrast the files of the N. Y. Tribune for August, September and October of 1856, with the Tribune of August, September, and October, 1860. And my purpose in this *exposé*,
at this time, and in this way, is that your Excellency may
realize, as I do with a sick heart, how *utterly abandoned* the
wretched people in Kansas are at this trying and terrible
hour, with a cold winter just upon them. My purpose is to
induce the Executive of this nation to adopt some plan for
the relief of a starving people, additional to the mere postponement of the land sales; for even this postponement will
not put bread in their mouths.

Seeing that the press of the country will do nothing effectual for them at this fearful crisis; seeing that only extraordinary remedies can reach so extraordinary a case, I come
to your Excellency as the proper source, and ask for some
official action, I care not what it is, so that speedy relief may
reach a multitude of starving American citizens, even though
they cannot vote.

Your Excellency can surely get these dreadful facts before

the country in a way to awaken sympathy, and insure aid, though I am powerless to do it. And this is my prayer.

But if the Executive of this great nation should, in his better judgment and broader knowledge, see no way for him to succeed where an humble citizen has failed, I shall then have but one resource left; I can make only one effort more. But this I must make, for having moved thus far and awakened the expectations of the starving, it is impossible that I should now desert them until the last promise has faded from the heavens; until my own heart with theirs has utterly died out. One last hope remains; it is that the people of another Government, and in another hemisphere, may take compassion upon starving Americans, as in former years of misfortune Americans took compassion upon them.

I am, sir, very respectfully, yours,

THADDEUS HYATT.

www.ingramcontent.com/pod-product-compliance
Lightning Source LLC
Chambersburg PA
CBHW020253090426
42735CB00010B/1904